720-972-5780

Emily Griffith
Opportunity's Teacher

Emily Griffith
Opportunity's Teacher

A NOW YOU KNOW BIO

Joyce B. Lohse

Coyote Ridge Elementary School
13770 Broadlands Drive
Broomfield CO 80023
720-972-5780

Filter Press, LLC
Palmer Lake, Colorado

to
Charlie Lohse

Library of Congress Cataloging-in-Publication Data

Lohse, Joyce B. (Joyce Burke), 1950-
  Emily Griffith : Opportunity's teacher / Joyce B. Lohse.
    p. cm. -- (A now you know bio)
  Includes bibliographical references and index.
  ISBN-13: 978-0-86541-077-0 (paper back : alk. paper)
  1. Griffith, Emily, ca. 1880-1947--Juvenile literature. 2. Teachers--United States--Biography--Juvenile literature. 3. Emily Griffith Opportunity School (Denver, Colo.)--Juvenile literature. I. Title. II. Series.
  LA2317.G668L65 2005
  371.1'0092--dc22
                                  2005023186

Cover photo courtesy Joyce B. Lohse.

Copyright © 2005 Joyce B. Lohse

All rights reserved. No part of this publication may be reproduced or transmitted in any form or by any means, electronic or mechanical, including photocopy, recording, or any information storage and retrieval system, without permission in writing from the publisher. Contact Filter Press, LLC at 888.570.2663.

Filter Press, LLC, P.O. Box 95, Palmer Lake, Colorado.

Printed in the United States of America

Contents

1 A Young Schoolteacher 1

2 Westward to Denver 8

3 Opportunity Is Born 12

4 Success and Rewards 24

5 Retirement Years 30

6 A Tragic End 34

Timeline 41

Glossary 44

Bibliography 47

Index 49

The Emily Griffith Opportunity School and its founder.

1 A Young Schoolteacher

Early in life, Emily Griffith knew she wanted to be a schoolteacher. To achieve her goal, she would overcome poverty, family difficulties, and meager formal education. Her intelligence and persistence would help her attain her goals. Emily would not let anybody tell her she was not capable of achieving her objectives. She knew she would succeed. With eager determination, she confronted her challenges and pursued her dreams, while improving the lives of countless people along the way.

Emily K. Griffith's life began near Cincinnati, in southern Ohio. Her mother, Martha, was in frail health, and her father, Andrew W., walked with a handicap. Andrew and Martha had a son and three daughters: Charles, Emily, Florence, and Ethelyn. Emily was the oldest daughter. Her sister, Florence, was mentally challenged. Two more children born into the Griffith family did not survive infancy.

Emily Griffith had two birth dates. February 10, 1868, was her real birthday, but for a long time, nobody could prove it. Emily's other birth date was 1880. Her listing in the 1880 and 1885 **U.S. Census records** led one author, Yale Huffman, to believe 1868 was the correct year. An 1870 census record, listing Emily Griffith as a two-year-old, confirmed her year of birth as 1868. Throughout her life, she never revealed her age.

It was common in the reserved **Victorian era** of the late 1800s for women to be secretive about their ages, in an attempt to appear younger. In Emily's case, she might have tampered with her age to obtain a teaching position. The tale she always told was that she began teaching school in 1894 as a teenager in a sod schoolhouse on the Nebraska prairie. Part of the story is true. She did begin teaching as a teenager, but the year was closer to sometime between 1884 and 1887, not 1894 as she stated. Whenever it began, her early teaching experience was the beginning of a lifelong dream to create a school for all who wished to learn.

Her family was far from wealthy. Money was scarce, and life was a constant struggle. While the family lived in Ohio, Emily's father worked as a lawyer. When that did not work out, he became a missionary, but with little success. Discouraged and restless, he made plans to move the family west.

In 1884, Andrew Griffith took his family across the **Great Plains** to Nebraska, hoping their prospects would improve. When the family arrived near the small town of Arnold in Custer County, Andrew decided this was the place he would try homesteading on the open prairie. He would claim the land to build his home, raise his family, and become a farmer.

Emily Griffith was a good student and quick to learn. Her schooling was spotty and often interrupted by her unsettled family, but she read and studied on her own to enhance her knowledge.

A story about her uncle who operated a ferryboat on the Erie Canal intrigued Emily. Whenever he docked his boat, he taught reading to others. He hung a lantern to shine over a homemade sign that invited "All Who Wish To Learn" to come aboard his boat. This story impressed young Emily, and the words from the sign stayed with her. "All Who Wish To Learn" would one day be the motto of a school she would establish.

Once they arrived in Nebraska, the Griffith family was no better off. The family decided that Emily must go to work. She was bright and capable, and through the years, her family relied on her to support them. She applied for a teaching job in the town of Broken Bow in the sod schoolhouse she had briefly attended herself.

As a young woman competing against experienced teachers for a job teaching children, Emily had little chance of being hired. The skeptical school board members asked to interview her before the board. When she was asked to read, she complied using her beautiful reading voice for which she was well known throughout her career.

After she passed the reading test, a school board member tested her spelling skills by asking her to spell **vicissitudes,** a tough word. After a moment of thought, she correctly spelled v-i-c-i-s-s-i-t-u-d-e-s. Not easily won over, the board member asked her to make up a math problem involving bushels of grain. With some thinking, Emily created a problem and its correct solution.

When she was asked to write something on the chalkboard, there was more to prove. She wrote, "I would like very much to teach in this school." One man, not yet convinced, did not like the way Emily wrote the letter *s*. She quickly removed the offending letter, then created a different kind of *s*. He liked that one. Emily finally earned the teaching position at the Broken Bow sod schoolhouse.

Life was far from easy for the new teacher. The common practice of the time was for teachers to live in the homes of their pupils, moving from house to house, one week after another. The families were poor, but provided food and shelter as best they could, which often meant sharing beds and stretching sparse meals. She spent spare time reading books so she could stay ahead of her students.

Emily had a bright, enthusiastic outlook, and got along well with her students. She learned important teaching skills as well as lessons in life while her students learned their school lessons from her. She soon realized that many of her pupils' parents lacked basic education. Some were immigrants from other countries who spoke and understood little or no English. This made a big impression on her. Perhaps this was the start of her dream to create a school for all who wished to learn, and of the educational theories she later developed. After all, how could her students learn when their parents as role models struggled with basic skills and **cultural literacy.**

Emily during her first years of teaching. After her death, many people remembered her fondly for her many kind and unselfish acts, and for the thousands who benefited from attending her Opportunity School.

Emily earned the respect of the community with her quick thinking. One day, a tornado rushed toward the little schoolhouse while the teacher and students were inside. Elinor Bluemel told the story in her biography, *Emily Griffith and the Opportunity School of Denver*. After Emily lined up the children under the solid center roof beam, she led them singing church hymns to keep them calm and occupied while the wind swirled and the walls toppled around them. Miraculously, no one was hurt, although the building had to be rebuilt.

A wood stove heated the sod schoolhouse. It was the only source of heat during brutally cold prairie winters. Boys took turns arriving at school early to start the stove fire for their young teacher. During classes, scarves, hats, mittens, and boots dried out by the stove, while the

Emily Griffith first taught school as a teenager in a schoolhouse made of sod bricks and a grass roof similar to this one near Broken Bow, Nebraska.

children tried to stay warm and thawed from the cold as they worked on their lessons.

Homesteaders had a hard time growing crops. Rainstorms were unpredictable, as were droughts and tornadoes. Grasshoppers ate the wheat and corn crops. With very few trees to provide wood, women and children collected buffalo chips, dried cowpies, and corn husks to burn for fuel. These hardy settlers were warned by those who arrived ahead of them to be prepared to face the challenges, or move on.

2 Westward to Denver

In 1895, Emily's father was tired of the struggles of farming and the hardships of prairie life. He felt it was time to move on to try to make a better living elsewhere. Packing up all they owned, the family moved once again. This time their destination was Denver, Colorado.

When they reached Denver, Emily's family again expected her to earn her way as a teacher, and to support the family. She applied for a job in the Denver Public Schools. Emily's lack of higher education made it hard for her to find a job. A determined young lady, Emily set out to convince another reluctant school board that she was a capable teacher.

When she approached the school district for a job, she said emphatically, "I AM GOING TO TEACH IN THE DENVER SCHOOLS." In spite of her spotty educational background, she asked only that she be allowed to prove herself, for she knew she could teach. She soon proved her abilities.

Emily was offered a position as an alternate teacher for the sixth grade at Central School. Her determination and positive attitude once again allowed her to gain a foothold in the school system. Her family settled in a neighborhood nearby, a poor area with immigrants from different countries.

The 1896 Denver School Superintendent's Report listed Emily Griffith on the roster of teachers. She was allowed to teach for three months at Central School, with a monthly salary of $60. The average teacher's salary that year was $119.68. Although her salary was low, it was a start.

A year later, Emily Griffith had full teaching status at Central School. Her students later remembered her as a most satisfactory teacher. Her skills developed along with her experience and awareness of the needs of those around her and in her community. She recognized that many people in her underprivileged neighborhood were immigrants with poor English and little education, similar to her neighbors in Nebraska.

Emily Griffith had close relationships with her students and continued to learn much about them and their families. Her students' parents had difficulty reading, writing, and figuring out how to pay their bills. A plan for helping was forming in her mind. Why should learning be for children only? Adults, too, needed education, especially those in poor neighborhoods. If parents improved their own education, perhaps they could help their children stay in school and achieve better jobs and lives themselves.

Emily continued to teach at Central School until 1904. At that time, she was assigned to the state education department and named assistant state superintendent for public instruction for all schools in Colorado. Although her work kept her out of the classroom, she occasionally visited schools and observed students. She was especially interested in knowing what caused some students to have difficulties learning. Her ongoing goal was to find ways to help people in the community achieve a better education, to make the most of their potential.

Four years later, Emily returned to the work she loved—teaching in the classroom. She taught eighth grade at the Twenty-Fourth Street School in the Five Points Neighborhood in Denver. For two more years, she taught at the school, learning about the needs of her students and their families and their daily struggles. She often visited other schools in the area, and teachers welcomed her advice. She continued to live in the home of her parents, who had moved to 1633 Humboldt Street in Denver. Her youngest sister, Ethelyn, was married to Herbert Willis, and they, too, lived with the Griffith family.

Emily was again appointed deputy superintendent of public instruction in 1910. On July 27, 1911, the State

Normal School and Teacher's College in Greeley awarded Emily a diploma and two Bachelor of **Pedagogy** degrees, which were licenses to teach in the public schools of Colorado for life. It was official. After more than seventeen years of teaching and education, Emily Griffith finally received her certified teacher's degrees.

At the Twenty-Fourth Street School, the problems of poverty and **truancy** kept students from learning. Her community of "folks," as she referred to the people of many nationalities who surrounded her, needed help. She wondered all the while, what could she do for them?

Emily knew there was a way to help. She observed, learned, and discussed educational methods with friends and colleagues. She began teaching night school classes during the only free time she and her adult students had.

An attractive, intelligent woman, Emily had no time in her busy schedule for interested **suitors,** although there were a few with serious intentions. Her life was full with her dedication to teaching and her family, and she never married.

The 1915 Denver City Directory listed Emily's occupation as a teacher at the Twenty-Fourth Street School, living at 1521 Fillmore Street, her father's home. She lived there for the next two **decades.** Soon, she was promoted to the position of principal at the Twenty-Fourth Street School.

3 Opportunity Is Born

Frances "Pinky" Wayne, a newspaper feature reporter and columnist, was Emily's friend for thirty years. On June 20, 1947, the *Rocky Mountain News* printed a tribute article to Emily Griffith's memory written by Pinky Wayne. In it, Pinky described a discussion with Emily at her newspaper office before Christmas 1915. Clothing and toys had been collected for children in the poor sections of town. Emily was there to help divide and distribute Christmas gifts.

As she organized the donations, Emily said to the reporter, "I wonder if you will let me tell you of a hope I have for the people in and out of my school—the boys and girls, their parents, too, whose education has been limited by poverty?

"I want to help to establish a school where the clock will be stopped from morning until midnight. I want the age limit for admission lifted and the classes so organized that a boy or girl working in a bakery, store, laundry or any kind of a shop who has an hour or two to spare may come to school, study what he or she wants to learn to make life more useful. The same rule goes for older folks too. I know I will be laughed at, but what of it? I already have a name for that school. It is **Opportunity."**

The dream had progressed to spoken words. This was the beginning of Emily's Opportunity School. It was a bold new idea. In Pinky Wayne, Emily found a powerful **ally** and enthusiastic supporter. Pinky was convinced that Emily's Opportunity School was a wonderful idea and would be an asset to the community, and she helped introduce it to the public.

The dream took shape. Emily pushed ahead and prepared to present her idea to the Board of Education, who resisted the idea of **adult education** at first. She said, "I'm trembling like a leaf because perhaps I am too ambitious. For myself, I really want nothing. I would expect no more than I am receiving as principal of Twenty-Fourth Street School because this is just an experiment."

On May 11, 1916, the Denver school board endorsed the Opportunity School. The school board accepted the idea of the school, and the condemned Longfellow School, at 13th and Welton Streets, was selected as the location for Emily's **non-traditional school.** The school district felt they had nothing to lose by turning the aging

The Emily Griffith Opportunity School photographed in the 1940s. The Longfellow School building was in poor condition when the Opportunity School moved in. Emily and her staff helped clean, paint, and repair it.

building over to Emily Griffith for her radical new experiment. It was no small task to prepare the building for use by students. Emily and her staff of five teachers spent the summer scrubbing, washing, painting, and making repairs. On September 9, 1916, Opportunity School was ready to open.

Opportunity School's doors opened, and if Emily feared nobody would show up, she need not have worried. Fourteen hundred students registered the first week. Just as the sign on her uncle's boat had welcomed "All

Who Wish To Learn," Emily's school welcomed students with her own sign and the same message: *For All Who Wish To Learn.* Principal Emily Griffith pushed her desk into the hallway and waited by the doorway to greet each student. It was the beginning of a new **tradition.**

The new school was open thirteen hours a day, five days a week. Students were allowed to attend walk-in classes at the school for an hour or two as their work schedules permitted. Subjects ranged from **telegraphy** to industrial **millinery,** from typewriting on the school's one typewriter to English for foreign language-speaking immigrants.

It seemed everybody wanted to enroll in a different subject, but they all wanted to learn. As they entered the building, Emily asked each student what subject they wished to study. A man wanted training in sign making. A foreign-born person wished to improve his English-speaking skills. A waitperson from a restaurant needed to improve his math **proficiency.**

Ladies who wished to learn needlework and sewing were encouraged to apply their skills to hat making for industrial millinery. Students wanted classes in cooking and carpentry. Young people who had quit school to take jobs to help their families earn money wanted to finish their basic academic education in evening classes.

Opportunity School allowed adults and children to learn different skills and **vocations** all at the same time.

STUDENTS Who Have Registered at Denver's Newest Educational Innovation—the Opportunity School. Left to Right—Miss Wynne Frake, Who Has Entered the Shorthand Class, and Wong Silk, Chinese Student in the Eighth Grade.

The Denver Times *published this photograph of two students from Emily Griffith's Opportunity School on opening day, September 6, 1916. An article with the headline, "1,500 Expected in Opportunity Classes Here," accompanied the photo.*

It was possible for workers to attend walk-in classes and evening sessions whenever their busy schedules allowed. **Aliens** from other countries were encouraged to study what they needed to know to become American citizens. Teaching methods were individualized and all classes were free of charge. Rules and disciplinary action were kept to a minimum, with total emphasis on achievement.

Emily Griffith continued to place her desk in the hallway by the door so she was accessible to greet her students and answer their questions. In that way, Emily kept close track of her students' needs. The chalkboard held messages for all who entered the school, starting with, "YOU CAN DO IT." Messages contained directions and useful information as well as **inspiration** for all who entered. "We do not believe in failure," she often said. She would print such a motto on a banner or sign to display in a place where everyone could see it. Another sign said, "Help One Another."

From the beginning, Opportunity School was a success. During the first year, 2,398 students attended and the faculty grew from five to thirty-eight teachers. The school was unusual in so many ways that it attracted a good deal of attention. Educators from other communities wanted to know how to start their own opportunity school.

A press release from the Denver Public Schools archives contained these words from Emily Griffith:

> **Know More!**
>
> **Inspiration** – Tales of Emily Griffith's kindness and encouragement are legendary. According to teacher and author Francell Lee Schrader, whose mother was an early teacher at Opportunity School, the most remarkable thing about Emily Griffith was her tremendous faith and belief in her students. Emily believed all of her students could succeed, and she expressed her support by posting inspirational messages in the school. Banners read, "You can do it" and "Help one another." What inspirational message would you put on a banner? Make a sign or banner of your favorite inspirational saying or motto.

"The one thing that has made Opportunity School the institution it is is because we have looked on each person who comes in as an individual. I think there is an individual thing in every person. *It is the big thing to know the need of the person.* Students come to learn a new trade, improve skills for better jobs, or continue with the education they did not for one reason or another receive."

Resistance to the school's approach endured. Not everyone thought Opportunity School was a good idea. Some people thought it was too radical and unusual to be practical. However, on April 10, 1917, the state of Colorado passed a law allowing the school to continue as a public vocational, evening, and opportunity school, open to all people. As Emily put it, "We will just have this school and there will be no entrance requirements." Opportunity School was here to stay.

When Emily discovered a need, she found a way to fill it. If a student needed a ride home, she slipped a nickel for carfare into his or her hand along with a handshake to conceal the gift. One evening, a young boy fainted in an evening class. He had no time to eat between his job and evening school, and had grown faint. Emily quickly observed that he was not the only student who had no time or money to eat, or money for extra streetcar fare to go home for a meal.

Emily solved the problem. Her mother made a pot of soup at home, and her sister Florence carried it to the school on the streetcar. A new sign appeared at the door that read, "A bowl of soup is served in the basement from 5:30-7:30—FREE. This saves you time." From then on, students entered their classes well fed and ready to learn.

Once, when a woman observed Emily filling dishes of soup and serving them to students, she suggested that Emily could find better work elsewhere. Of course, the woman did not know she was speaking to the principal when she gave her well-meaning advice. Emily smiled in her kindly way and said she was happy where she was. She would not tell the woman she was principal of the school and risk embarrassing her.

A posed photograph shows students in the 1920s studying English, sewing, millinery, telegraphy, and typewriting. A wide variety of lessons and courses were taught at the Opportunity School.

The soup tradition continued. About two hundred bowls of soup were served each day. When a women's club heard about it, they took over providing meat for the soup. Every afternoon, Florence went to the school to serve soup. This unusual consideration for her students was one example of the kindness for which Emily Griffith was widely known and loved. Soup became a **symbol** of the sharing and caring attitude students found at Opportunity School.

By the second year, the school was alive with students, and the school developed according to their needs. The number of students had to be limited to those who needed instruction for their work or trade and to improve their lives. Those with a mild interest in their studies did not enroll. It was the beginning of World War I, and an auto repair shop was started to teach mechanics and steel work, and that area of study grew.

Emily was proud of students who served in the armed forces and fought for their country. She was proud of all of her students and found ways to show it. For instance, Emily was fond of wearing fancy hats. To show pride in her millinery students, she wore the hats they created wherever she went. Her support and enthusiasm never wavered.

Because she never married or had a family of her own, Emily considered the people at the school and in the community her family. If the Denver police found a young person without a home or an immigrant needing help getting established or who wished to learn English, they went to Emily for help. She quickly found those in need a place to stay and enrolled them in her school so they could learn the skills they needed to work and function within the community.

For years, Emily and Florence lived in their parents' two-story brick house on Fillmore Street near Colfax in Denver. They had settled in as part of the Capitol Hill neighborhood, where their father, Andrew, served as elder at the Capitol Heights Presbyterian Church.

In 1918, Emily's father died. Two years later, her mother died. Both were buried at Fairmount Cemetery

Emily took great pride in wearing hats created in millinery classes by students from the Opportunity School and was often photographed in them.

in Denver, in a plot purchased by Emily Griffith for seventy-five dollars. Her parents lived to see their daughter achieve her dreams and goals while they benefited continually from her care and financial support.

Emily and Florence continued to live in the brick house on Fillmore Street. Emily took care of her sister who was unable to live on her own. Florence returned her sister's loyalty with her companionship and help with projects such as making soup at the school. Their brother, Charles, lived in Denver with his family. Their sister, Ethelyn, sometimes called Ethel, lived in Denver, worked as a schoolteacher, and married a second time to a man named Evans Gurtner. At one point, she worked as a teacher at Emily's Opportunity School.

> **Know More!**
>
> **Hats and Millinery –**
> In the late 1800s and early 1900s, fancy hats worn by women were considered fashionable. Jobs in the millinery trade were filled by people, mostly women, who created and decorated hats. Emily Griffith liked to wear different styles of hats.
>
> Point to ponder: What happened when bird feathers, plumage, and even entire birds were used to decorate thousands of hats? Design or draw a fancy hat, that Emily would have enjoyed wearing.

4 Success and Rewards

Opportunity School continued to succeed. As its founder and principal, Emily Griffith became well known. She was often asked to share her instructional methods and plans for school management. Invitations to speak came from all over the United States and abroad. Emily did not accept many of these invitations. According to Pinky Wayne, she would laugh and say, "What would I do so far from home?" She wanted to work uninterrupted at her beloved school.

Many organizations honored Emily Griffith. In 1920, the Kiwanis Club of Denver invited her to join their organization. This was more than an honor. It was a special tribute. At the time, she was the only woman invited to join any Kiwanis Club. The Kiwanians recognized her achievements throughout her life.

Emily Griffith was elected president of the Colorado Education Association in 1922. It was an honor and a challenge for the Opportunity School principal to be selected to lead all educators and school administrators in the state of Colorado. The announcement was made at the Colorado Education Association convention that year, attended by 6,500 people.

Emily Griffith started other projects intended to help the community. For many years, Emily tried to help homeless people. Many of the homeless were young boys. In 1927, she once again filled a need to help by starting Number 9 Pearl Street in Denver, "a home for a boy who needs one." It provided a safe place where **displaced** boys could sleep and stay—and consider it a home. Today, the agency is called

EMILY GRIFFITH.

Emily had been nominated by Colorado Governor William E. Sweet for the $25,000 Wilson Foundation Award for her public service when the Rocky Mountain News published this photograph in 1923.

Denver Post publisher F.G. Bonfils presents Emily with Colorado's No. one license plate.

the Griffith Centers for Children, located in Larkspur, with branches in Rifle and Colorado Springs, Colorado.

A *Denver Post* article on January 31, 1932, reported how Emily found another way to help the community with education. Students hospitalized for long periods of time at Children's Hospital, with illnesses such as polio, needed to continue their studies. If they could not get to school, Opportunity School would come to them. Emily supervised educational lessons and vocational training programs that helped student-patients prepare for jobs and further studies once they were able to leave the hospital.

In December 1931, Emily was presented with a merit award from the *Denver Post,* in cooperation with the Colorado secretary of state for her service to education and humanity. She received the Colorado license plate No. 1 in a ceremony presided over by F. G. Bonfils, publisher of the *Denver Post.*

According to an article in the *Denver Post* on December 4, 1931:

> No citizen of Colorado presents a record of such continuous, unselfish service as Emily Griffith, quiet and unassuming, who had the courage to light a new torch in the world of education and pass it on to those who, save for her vision, might have remained unaware of their capabilities and their place in the world.

In 1916, she presented her plan for a clockless, ageless school to the Denver school board. All day long the doors of the school, she planned, should be open so boys and girls, men and women, regardless of age or race or creed, might use what time they had to increase their education. Out of her own pocket, she provided materials for a soup room where those who worked during the day at small wages might have an evening meal without the expense of going home and returning to the school. She specialized in courses that would help students become more efficient craftsmen, and again and again she has backed her faith in a student with money she could ill afford to loan.

And over the door to the school she had chiseled the all-embracing word **OPPORTUNITY.**

Although Emily continued to manage the school, she was growing tired. It was time for her to hand over management of Opportunity School. Emily Griffith retired from teaching on December 12, 1933. Would the school be able to carry on without her unwavering personal attention? Only time would tell.

With her carefully selected staff trained over the years, her teaching and management methods were firmly established. Due to her foresight and planning, the school would endure and thrive without her.

On March 14, 1934, Opportunity School's name was changed in her honor. Dr. A. L. Thelkeld, Superintendent of Denver Schools, suggested the name be changed to the Emily Griffith Opportunity School, as it is known to this day. Although she resisted the name change at first, Emily eventually gratefully accepted the honor.

Founder Emily Griffith cuts the cake at a twenty-first birthday party for the Emily Griffith Opportunity School, in 1938. She is joined at the happy celebration by Superintendent of Schools, Dr. Alexander Stoddard (left); Opportunity School Principal, Paul Essert (near right); and Opportunity School Assistant Principal, Mrs. Mary Miller (far right).

5 Retirement Years

Emily moved to Pinecliffe, Colorado, a beautiful, heavily wooded, picturesque community a few miles from the town of Nederland, at the border of Boulder and Pitkin counties. Her sister Ethelyn's husband, Evans Gurtner, had bought several plots of land in Pinecliffe. Years before her retirement, Emily bought four lots in rural Pinecliffe for two hundred dollars.

Emily wished to live out her years in her quiet cabin in the woods. She led a simple life in a rustic cabin built for her by a colleague from the Opportunity School. Friends in the community combined efforts to help improve the cabin and her living conditions. Emily beat a coffee can with a stick to call and gather neighbors for friendly chats on the banks of South Boulder Creek. Former students made a point of keeping in touch with her, and many visited from time to time.

The honors and notice continued. The story of Emily's teaching career and the Opportunity School caught the attention of Ernie Pyle, a famous journalist, and was the subject of one of his widely read newspaper columns. Most of the time, Emily stayed secluded in her mountain home with Florence, whose health was declining, and their dog, a spaniel named Chips. She accepted only fifty dollars a month as a teacher's retirement pension, even though she was entitled to an administrator's pension of one hundred dollars.

Emily Griffith is standing in the doorway of her rustic cabin in Pinecliffe, Boulder County, Colorado, where she lived in retirement from 1934 to 1947.

A spaniel named Chips was Emily Griffith's dog companion at her Pinecliffe cabin. This photo of Chips at the cabin appeared in the Denver Post shortly after Emily's death.

Her friends were unhappy that Emily's living conditions were so primitive. She wanted to lead a quiet, simple life, so she turned down offers of a modern house and living conditions. After years of protests, she accepted help from friends and added electricity and plumbing to the cabin.

Emily Griffith was used to paying her own way. The following letter to the Kiwanis Club of Denver shows her independent and self-reliant spirit.

Pinecliffe, Colo.
Dec. 2, 1946

Kiwanis Club of Denver
Mr. Jack E. Beatty
Officers and Directors

Dear Friends,
    Your wonderful thought of making my home more comfortable and pleasant has materialized. The gift is perfect in every particular and I am very happy.
    Knowing that you would permit me to be very frank I want to tell you how I feel. I must do my part, and as the gift is now a part of my home. I must pay what you have expended, which I could never have secured especially when equipment and labor is so difficult to secure. You understand what I am trying to say, but is difficult to put in words.
    Always you have been my close friends and now you have added greatly to my comfort. Please let me be on good terms with myself, and let me know the amount of the expenditures.
    The debt I owe for your expressed belief in me during the years at Opportunity can never be paid.

Very sincerely,
Emily Griffith

6 A Tragic End

On June 18, 1947, life ended abruptly for Emily and Florence. Denver residents were saddened and shocked when they read in the newspaper on June 19, 1947, that the Griffith sisters had been murdered in their mountain cabin. Fred Lundy, a friend who lived nearby, was immediately suspected of shooting them. A month later, his body was found nearby in South Boulder Creek. His death was ruled a suicide by drowning. Although speculation continues, Lundy's involvement has not been proven and the crime was never solved.

Emily was widely missed and mourned by hundreds of friends and admirers who gathered in the pouring rain outside Central Presbyterian Church in Denver for her funeral. Normally busy classrooms were silenced at the Emily Griffith Opportunity School, which was closed for the funeral that day. Kiwanis Club members and school officials delivered Emily's **eulogy** and carried the caskets. They spoke of Emily's "nobleness of nature, gentleness of character and faith, and her spirit that will never die."

Many stories of Emily's generosity were shared following her death. A colleague from the school remembered "standing by the door with her as pupils left night school to make sure that each had carfare and a place to sleep." Close friends recalled that she was always warm and friendly, the favorite in any group. She was admired for

Emily and her sister Florence share a gravesite in Denver's Fairmount Cemetery. Beneath Emily's name on the headstone is the inscription, "Founder Opportunity School – For all who wish to learn."

her belief that "even the most incorrigible youngster, given an opportunity and enough encouragement, would turn out pretty well."

Emily Griffith's legacy lives on and memories of her work in education endure, as well as memories of her kindness, spirit, and sense of humor. The Emily Griffith Opportunity School continued and endured, and operates today as a fitting **memorial** bearing her name. Her once-criticized teaching theories, based on an individualized approach to each student's abilities, are now more widely accepted.

The Emily Griffith Opportunity School, at 12th and Welton Streets in Denver, eighty-eight years after welcoming its first students.

Since Opportunity School opened its doors in 1916, over one and a half million people have enrolled to learn and improve their lives. In 1949, a four-story addition was built. Today the school takes up more than a city block in downtown Denver, at 12th and Welton Streets. Vocational training and basic education are offered to 13,000 students each year in 350 subjects. There are 350 people working at the school, and sixty community advisory committees are available as consultants.

Classes continue throughout the year, day and night. Emily's words, keeping her spirit alive, are quoted in the class roster: "We do not believe in failure." Classes include high school and adult basic education, a variety of health occupations, accounting, computer and office skills, power plant mechanics, automotive repair, custodial services, carpentry, construction, repairing, and welding. The days of millinery classes are past, but fashion and floral design, culinary arts, and child care are taught.

Emily's other projects continue on as well. Number 9 Pearl Street, now known as the Griffith Centers for Children, located in Larkspur, Rifle, and Colorado Springs, are still **sanctuaries** for children who need direction.

In 1976, Emily Griffith's memory was honored when a stained glass window portrait was placed in Colorado's state capitol, for all visitors to see. Her window was

A stained glass portrait of Emily was installed in the Colorado State Capitol in 1976 as a tribute to her. Coloradans are chosen for this honor by the Colorado State Senate to acknowledge a significant contribution.

placed in the hallway outside the senate chambers because she was not directly involved in government. The cost to build and install the window was $4,500.

In 2000, fifty-two years after her death, Mayor Wellington Webb issued Denver's Millennium Award for Denver's Most Useful Citizen to Emily Griffith. Her memory lives on, as those who value education will never forget her contributions to learning in Colorado and to her school, "For Those Who Wish To Learn."

Each year, Emily Griffith Opportunity School celebrates Emily's birthday. The celebration takes place at her gravesite in Denver's Fairmount Cemetery. Children from a nearby elementary school join in the party. The children learn about life and customs of a century ago. They create **nosegays** to lay at Emily's gravestone, sing songs, play games, and enjoy eating treats made by Emily Griffith

Historian Debra Faulkner performs as Emily Griffith for school children at Fairmount Cemetery. Emily's life is celebrated at the cemetery each year on her birthday.

Opportunity School culinary students. A storyteller dressed as Emily Griffith visits the group to tell them about Emily's life and the beginning of Opportunity School. It is a joyous and fitting celebration of a life well lived by a bright and beautiful person.

> **Know More!**
>
> **EGOS Today** – Study a list of classes from the Emily Griffith Opportunity School (EGOS), either with a printed copy of the course catalog, or on the Web site at: http://www.egos-school.com/Catalog/. Read descriptions of the classes. What classes would you like to take? What classes offered at Opportunity School when it first opened no longer need to be taught? Which are still needed for current schooling and work skills? What courses taught now were not available when the school first opened?

Timeline

1868 – Emily Griffith is born near Cincinnati, Ohio.

1884 – Emily's family moves to Nebraska.

1884-1887 – Emily [16-19] teaches school and lives with the families of her students.

1895 – The Griffith family moves to Denver, Colorado. Emily teaches school part-time.

1897 – Emily Griffith [28] earns full teaching status at Central School. She teaches sixth-, seventh-, and eighth-grade classes.

1904 – Emily [36] is named Deputy State Superintendent of Schools. She serves in this position for four years.

1908 – Emily begins teaching at Twenty-Fourth Street School in the Five Points Neighborhood.

1910 – Emily is appointed Deputy State Superintendent of Public Instruction for two years.

1911 – Emily [43] receives teaching diplomas from State Normal School and Teachers College of Colorado at Greeley. She continues to teach at Twenty-Fourth Street School.

1916 – On September 9, Opportunity School opens. Emily Griffith [48] is principal.

1920 – Emily Griffith is named the first honorary female member of the Kiwanis Club of Denver. Appointed to the State Child Welfare Board.

1922 – Emily [54] named president of the Colorado Education Association.

1926 – Expansion and new construction were completed on the Opportunity School building at 12th and Welton Streets.

1927 – Emily Griffith opens Number 9 Pearl Street, a residence for homeless boys, known today as the Griffith Centers for Children.

1933 – Emily Griffith [65] retires from her job as principal of the Opportunity School.

1933–1945 – Emily serves twelve years on the State Board of Vocational Education.

1934 – Opportunity School changes its name to Emily Griffith Opportunity School.

1947 – On June 18, Emily Griffith [79] is murdered in her mountain cabin in Pinecliffe.

1972 – Emily Griffith Opportunity School registers its one-millionth student.

1976 – A stained glass portrait of Emily Griffith is dedicated in the Colorado State Capitol.

1980 – Governor Richard Lamm proclaims February 8 Emily Griffith Day.

1985 – Emily Griffith is inducted into the Colorado Women's Hall of Fame.

2000 – Emily Griffith is recipient of Mayor Wellington Webb's Millennium Award for Denver's Most Useful Citizen.

Glossary

adult education – individualized instruction to teach adults basic skills to enhance their ability to perform work at a trade and for their personal cultural literacy

aliens – persons from different countries and cultural backgrounds

ally – a supportive friend or co-worker

cultural literacy – educational and artistic knowledge of a civilization, region, or society

decades – periods of ten years

displaced – a person with no place to live or no place to call home

eulogy – a speech presented during a funeral about the life of the deceased person

Great Plains – prairie grassland between the Mississippi River and the Rocky Mountains

homesteaders – farmers or settlers who obtained 160 acres, or one-quarter square mile, of free prairie land by fulfilling the requirements of the Homestead Act of 1862

inspiration – motivation with energy, optimism, and stimulation

memorial – a memory preserved by an object or written document

millinery – the art or practice of making hats, mostly for women

non-traditional school – education for students not served by the public schools

nosegays – flowers gathered in small bunches or bouquets often tied with a ribbon

opportunity – a chance for improvement; an occasion or circumstance made available at a favorable time

pedagogy – teaching of children by a schoolmaster (teacher)

proficiency – skill in a particular subject

sanctuaries – shelters offering comfort and protection

suitors – gentlemen interested in a social, or romantic, relationship

symbol – a significant sign or image

telegraphy – transmitting messages over a telegraph line using a system of dots and dashes for communication

tradition – ritual or practice passed from one generation to another

truancy – skipping school

U.S. Census records – data the United States government collects, approximately every decade, recording all people and households in the country

vicissitudes – changes or mutations; passing from one phase or condition to another

Victorian era – named for Queen Victoria of England, a period of time during the late 1800s in which style and conduct were especially restrained and conservative

vocations – professions or trades applied during employment

Bibliography

Abbott/Leonard/McComb, *Colorado: A History of the Centennial State,* University Press of Colorado, Niwot, Colo., 1982, pp. 370-371.

Ayer, Eleanor, H., *Colorado Chronicles v. 2— Famous Colorado Women,* Jende-Hagan Bookcorp, Frederick, Colo. 1982, pp. 26-29.

Bluemel, Elinor, *Emily Griffith and the Opportunity School of Denver,* 1954.

City Directories, Denver, Colorado, 1915.

Denver Post, November 13, 1922, p. 19.

Denver Post, March, 3, 1931, p. 6; December 4, 1931, p. 1.

Denver Post, January 1, 1932, p. 3.

Denver Post, April 28, 1940, p. 2.

Denver Post, June 19, 21-22, July 6, 1947.

Denver Public Schools archival letters, articles, and press releases regarding EGOS.

Emily Griffith Opportunity School, *Emily Griffith Story* (brochure).

Emily Griffith Opportunity School, Class Roster, 2004.

Fairmount Cemetery (booklet), *Distinguished Colorado Women Walking Tour,* Denver, Colorado, 1997, Item #2.

Fay, Abbott, *Famous Coloradans,* Mountaintop Books, Paonia, Colo., 1990, p. 94.

Huffman, Yale, *The Life and Death of Emily Griffith,* Denver Westerner's Roundup, 1989.

Noel, Thomas J., *The Colorado Almanac,* West Winds Press, Portland, Ore., 2001, pp. 98, 127.

Nostalgia Magazine, Sept./Oct. 1988, Vol. 5, No. 5.

Opportunity News, April 1945, Vol. V, Number 8.

Opportunity News, April 1946, Vol. VII, Number 2.

Rocky Mountain News, December 30, 1918, Obituary for Andrew Griffith, p. 9.

Rocky Mountain News, November 13, 1922, p. 2.

Rocky Mountain News, April 15, 1924, p. 7; April 26, 1924, p. 14; April 27, 1924, p. 8.

Rocky Mountain News, June 20-22, 1947.

Rocky Mountain News, December 8, 1949, p. 5, 9.

Ubbelohde/Benson/Smith, *A Colorado History,* Pruett Publishing Co., Boulder, Colo., pp. 265-266.

University of Northern Colorado, State Normal School of Colorado, Commencement Program, July 24, 1911.

48 *Emily Griffith*

U.S. Census, 1870 and 1880, Hamilton County, Ohio.
U.S. Census, 1885, Custer County, Nebraska.
U.S. Census, 1900 and 1910, Arapahoe County, Colo.
Welton Street Journal, February 1980, Vol. IX, No. 2

Web Sites

"Colorado State Capitol Virtual Tour," Emily Griffith Stained Glass Window
   http://www.colorado.gov/dpa/doit/archives/cap/egriff.htm
Dr. Colorado's Denver History – Emily Griffith
   http://www.denvergov.org/AboutDenver/history_char_griffith.asp
Emily Griffith Opportunity School – School History:
   http://www.egos-school.com/History
Griffith Centers for Children *http://www.emilygriffith.com/Frame.html*
Wichita State University Libraries – Department of Special Collections – Sod Houses
   http://specialcollections.wichita.edu/collections/ms/95-20/sodhouse.html

Other Resources

Colorado Historical Society, Denver, Colorado, Emily Griffith MSS Box #1514 (Contains letters from Emily Griffith, Fairmount Cemetery deeds, and land deeds in Pinecliffe, Colorado.)
Colorado State Archives, Denver, Colorado, 1896 Superintendent's Report, microfilm S86, Roll 6, Arapahoe County Schools, p. 8.
Denver Public School Archives, Denver, Colorado, house organs and press releases, visited August 5, 2004.
Emily Griffith Opportunity School, Denver, Colorado, visited January 15, 2004.
Emily Griffith Opportunity School, Denver, Colorado, visited June 22, 2004.
Fairmount Cemetery, Denver, Colorado, visited February 10 and July 12, 2004.
Pinecliffe, Colorado, visited July, 10, 2004.
University of Northern Colorado, Michener Library Archives, Greeley, Colorado.

Index

Broken Bow, Nebraska, 3, 4, 5, 7

Capitol Heights Presbyterian Church, 21
Central Presbyterian Church, 34
Central School, 9, 10
Children's Hospital, 26-27
Colorado Education Association, 24, 25
Colorado State Capitol, 37, 38, 39

Denver, Colorado, 8.
Denver Post, 26, 27-28
Denver Public Schools, 8, 10, 13, 17

Faulkner, Debra, 39

Griffith, Andrew (father), 1, 2, 3, 21-22
Griffith, Emily, birth dates, 2; death, 34; Opportunity founder, 13-14; Opportunity principal, 15, 17-19; retirement, 28,30; siblings, 1, 23; teaching career, 2, 3, 4, 6, 9, 10,11.
Griffith, Florence (sister), 1, 20, 21, 23, 31, 34, 35
Griffith, Martha (mother), 1, 3, 22
Gurtner, Ethelyn Griffith (sister), 1, 10, 23, 30

Kiwanis Club, 24, 32, 33, 34

Number 9 Pearl Street (Griffith Centers for Children), 25-26, 37

Opportunity School (Emily Griffith Opportunity School), 13-15, 16, 17, 20, 24, 27, 28, 29

Pinecliffe, Colorado, 30

Sod dwellings, 2, 3, 6

Twenty-Fourth Street School, 10, 11

Wayne, Frances "Pinky", 12, 13, 24

Acknowledgments

Filter Press recently launched *Now You Know Bios*, a series of biographies for young people. I am proud they have embraced my work as worthy of inclusion. Kari Gomez-Smith, public relations manager for the Emily Griffith Opportunity School, graciously shared stories, photos, and the spirit of Emily's Opportunity School. Susan Oakes, librarian, continues to monitor, cheer, and bolster me with valuable observations and treasured friendship. Terri Weiss, librarian, lent helpful insights about nonfiction elements, then continued to support and believe. Nancy Niero, historian at Fairmount Cemetery, helps conserve and preserve Emily's traditions. Debra Faulkner, historian, shared ideas generously and unselfishly. Tim Summers, Denver Public Schools Public Information Officer, guided me to archives, provided photos, and allowed me to study and absorb. Helpful resources and people abound at Denver Public Library's Western History Department, Colorado Historical Society, Colorado State Archives, the Rocky Mountain Region National Archives, and the University of Northern Colorado's Michener Library. My dear husband, family, and friends energize me with their support and encouragement. Women Writing the West provides road maps and role models. I thank you all.

The Author

Award-winning author Joyce B. Lohse grew up in Illinois, where she sometimes spent her school recess time writing stories and poems. She is the author of a dual biography of Colorado's first governor and his wife entitled, *First Governor, First Lady: John and Eliza Routt of Colorado*, and *Justina Ford, Medical Pioneer*. She is happiest when researching and writing about the women of the West. Learn more about Joyce Lohse and her work at www.lohseworks.com.